Rome Long Ago

by Michael Ryall

Table of Contents

Introduction 2
Chapter 1 What Was Ancient Rome? 4
Chapter 2 Who Were Roman Citizens? 10
Chapter 3 What Was Life Like in Ancient Rome? . . 16
Chapter 4 What Happened to Ancient Rome? 22
Summary 28
Glossary 30
Index 32

Introduction

This book is about **Rome** long ago. This book is about **ancient** Rome.

Ancient Rome had a **civilization**. A civilization is a group of people. The people share ideas about living together.

▲ People lived in Ancient Rome.

Read about the Roman civilization.

Words to Know

 ancient

 citizens

 civilization

 Colosseum

 emperor

 empire

 gladiators

 republic

 Rome

See the Glossary on page 30.

Chapter 1

What Was Ancient Rome?

Ancient Rome was a city at first. Rome was near a river. Rome was on seven hills. Rome was built about 750 B.C.

▲ Ancient Rome was a city.

DID YOU KNOW?

There is a famous story about Rome. Twin boys were floating down a river. The boys were Romulus and Remus. A wolf found the twins. She cared for them. The twins built a city when they grew up. The city was Rome.

People conquered ancient Rome about 600 B.C. These people were the Etruscans. Etruscans ruled ancient Rome. Then, the people of Rome made the Etruscans leave.

▲ This is a statue of an Etruscan.

Chapter 1

Rome started a new government about 510 B.C. The government was a **republic**. Romans chose representatives. The representatives controlled the government. The republic did not have a king.

▲ The Romans had a republic.

What Was Ancient Rome?

Rome wanted more land. Roman soldiers conquered many people. Rome controlled all of Italy. Then, Rome controlled land around the Mediterranean Sea.

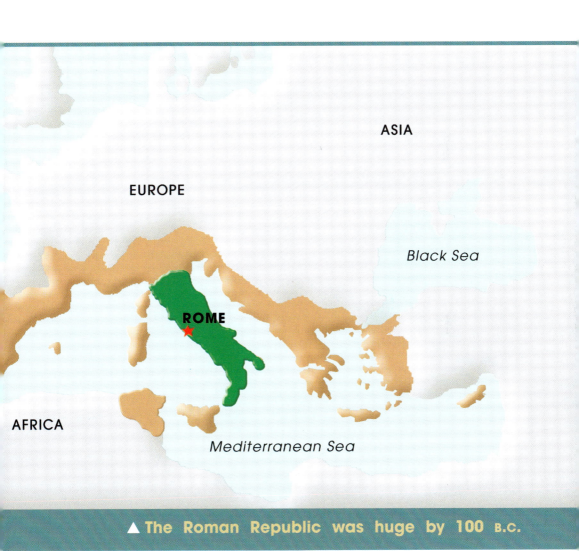

▲ The Roman Republic was huge by 100 B.C.

KEY
- Rome 275 B.C.
- Rome growth by 133 B.C.

Chapter 1

The Roman Republic had many problems. People fought against Rome. Army leaders controlled the government. Julius Caesar was an important army leader.

▲ Enemies stabbed Julius Caesar.

PEOPLE TO KNOW

Julius Caesar controlled the government. Caesar had enemies. The enemies stabbed Caesar to death.

What Was Ancient Rome?

Many people wanted power after Caesar died. A man named Octavian won power.

Octavian changed his name to Augustus. Octavian said he was **emperor** of Rome. An **empire** has an emperor. The Roman Republic was now the Roman Empire.

It's a Fact
The month of July is named for Julius Caesar. The month of August is named for Augustus.

▲ Augustus was the first emperor of Rome. An emperor is like a king.

Chapter 2

Who Were Roman Citizens?

Some Roman **citizens** were very rich. These citizens had power in the government. They were the leaders of the government.

▲ Citizens wore togas.

Rich citizens controlled one part of the government. Rich citizens controlled the Senate. The Senate was very powerful.

▲ The Senate was part of the government.

Chapter 2

Most Roman citizens were poor. Some poor citizens were farmers. Some poor citizens made things. Other poor citizens worked in shops.

▲ Poor citizens worked in this bakery.

Poor citizens wanted more power in the government. The poor citizens formed a group. The group had leaders. The leaders got more power for poor citizens.

▲ Poor citizens had leaders.

Chapter 2

Rome did not have written laws. The poor citizens wanted written laws. Rich citizens wrote the laws on twelve tablets. The tablets were the Twelve Tables.

▲ Romans had laws.

It's a Fact
One law said people had to pay debts. People could be slaves if they did not pay.

FIGURE IT OUT

Why did poor people want written laws?

Who Were Roman Citizens?

Women in Rome were citizens. Women could own property. Women could not be part of the government.

Slaves could not be citizens. Slaves could not be part of the government. Slaves could not own property.

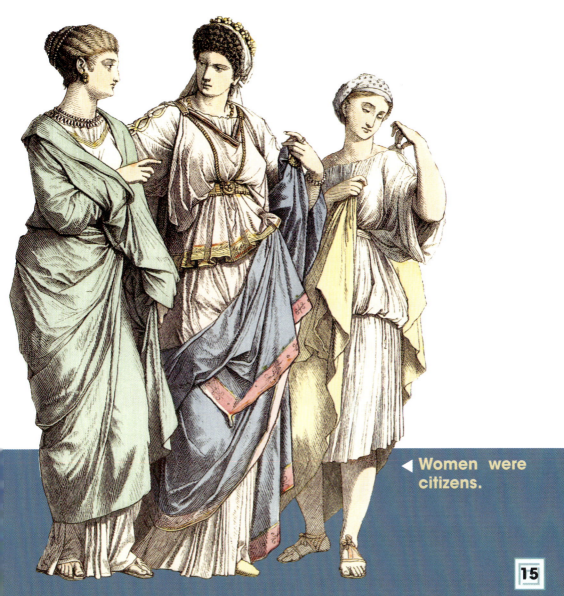

◀ Women were citizens.

Chapter 3

What Was Life Like in Ancient Rome?

Rich Roman people lived in large houses. The houses had water and indoor toilets. Fountains and gardens were outside the houses.

Rich people had feasts, or large meals. Servants worked for the rich people.

▲ Rich Romans had large houses.

Poor Roman people lived in apartment buildings. Often the apartment buildings fell down. Often the apartment buildings had fires.

Many poor families lived in one room. Often they did not have enough food.

THEN & NOW

Most apartments in ancient Rome did not have kitchens. Today, most apartments in Rome do have kitchens.

▲ Roman apartment buildings had shops on the bottom floor.

Chapter 3

Roman people went to theaters. The people watched plays and contests in the theaters.

The **Colosseum** was a theater in Rome. Rich people went to the Colosseum. Poor people went to the Colosseum, too.

▲ The Colosseum is still in Rome.

What Was Life Like in Ancient Rome?

Gladiators fought each other in the Colosseum. Sometimes the gladiators fought wild animals. Often the gladiators were slaves.

Sometimes people put water in the Colosseum. Small boats sailed on the water. People on the boats fought each other.

▲ Gladiators fought each other in the Colosseum.

It's a Fact
The Colosseum had seats for about 50,000 people.

▲ Gladiators fought wild animals in the Colosseum.

Chapter 3

The Roman people built aqueducts. The aqueducts brought clean water to the city. The people built public baths. Many people washed in public baths.

▲ Romans built this aqueduct.

▲ Romans built this bath.

What Was Life Like in Ancient Rome?

Roman people built many roads. The roads had tunnels and bridges. The roads were built well. People drive on some of the roads today.

▲ The Appian Way is an ancient Roman road.

Chapter 4

What Happened to Ancient Rome?

Rome was an empire in 27 B.C. Roman governors helped rule the empire. People traveled through the empire on Roman roads.

CHRISTIANITY

Jesus was born in the Roman Empire. Jesus lived in the Roman Empire. Jesus preached in the Roman Empire. Christianity began in the Roman Empire.

▲ Roman governors were part of the empire.

Many soldiers guarded the Roman Empire. The emperor had to pay the soldiers. The emperor collected taxes to pay them. Many Roman people were too poor to pay taxes. The emperor could not collect enough taxes.

▲ Soldiers guarded the Roman Empire.

DID YOU KNOW?

Roman soldiers knew how to fight. They also built roads and bridges.

Chapter 4

The Roman Empire was huge. The emperor split the empire in two parts. There was a western Roman Empire. There was an eastern Roman Empire.

▲ Rome was the capital city of the western empire. Constantinople was the capital city of the eastern empire.

DID YOU KNOW?

The western Roman Empire had an emperor. The eastern Roman Empire had an emperor.

What Happened to Ancient Rome?

The western empire was weak. People invaded the western empire. People invaded the city of Rome. The western Roman Empire ended in 476 A.D.

▲ People attacked Rome.

DID YOU KNOW?
About one million people lived in Rome. Other people invaded Rome. Then, only about 20,000 people were in Rome.

Chapter 4

The eastern Roman Empire was strong. The eastern empire lasted for one thousand years. Emperors lived in Constantinople.

▲ Constantinople had walls.

What Happened to Ancient Rome?

Then & Now

Constantinople was the capital of the eastern empire. Today this city is Istanbul.

SOLVE THIS

Rome became an empire in 27 B.C. The western Roman Empire ended in 476 A.D. How long did the western part of the empire last?

Answer: 503 years

Summary

Ancient Rome had a great civilization. Ancient Rome was a republic. Ancient Rome ruled many lands. Finally, Ancient Rome was an empire.

TIME LINE OF ANCIENT ROME

About 750 B.C.	About 600 B.C.	About 510 B.C.
The city of Rome was built.	Etruscans conquered Rome.	Rome became a republic.

27 B.C.	About 284 A.D.	476 A.D.
Rome became an empire.	The Roman Empire split in two parts.	The western Roman Empire ended.

Think About It

1. Tell about the citizens of ancient Rome.
2. How did the Roman Republic become an empire?

Glossary

ancient very old

*Rome was an **ancient** civilization.*

citizens people who could be part of the government

*Rome had rich **citizens** and poor **citizens**.*

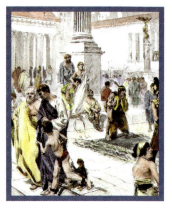

civilization a group of people that share ideas about living together

*Ancient Rome had a **civilization**.*

Colosseum an outdoor theater in Rome

*Gladiators fought in the **Colosseum**.*

emperor leader of the Roman Empire

*Augustus was the first **emperor** of Rome.*

empire lands ruled by an emperor

*Roman emperors ruled the **empire**.*

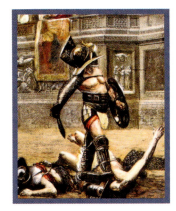  

gladiators people who fought animals and other gladiators

*The **gladiators** fought in the Colosseum.*

republic a civilization with a special government

*Rome was a **republic** for hundreds of years.*

Rome (1) a city (2) a republic (3) an empire

*First **Rome** was a city. Then **Rome** was a republic. Finally, **Rome** was an empire.*

Index

ancient, 2, 4–5, 21, 28–29
apartment buildings, 17
aqueducts, 20
Augustus, 9
Christianity, 22
citizens, 10–16
civilization, 2–3, 5, 28
Colosseum, 18–19
Constantinople, 24, 26–27
emperor, 9, 23–24, 26
empire, 9, 22, 24, 26–29
Etruscans, 5, 28
feasts, 16
gladiators, 19
government, 6, 8, 10–11, 13, 15
Jesus, 22
Julius Caesar, 8–9
laws, 14
Mediterranean Sea, 7
Octavian, 9
republic, 6–9, 28–29
roads, 21–23
Roman Empire, 9, 22–27, 29
Rome, 2, 4–9, 14–15, 22, 24–25, 27–29
Romulus and Remus, 4
slaves, 14–15, 19
soldiers, 7–8, 23
taxes, 23
women, 15